THE WINE AND WISDOM SERIES No.2

THE
LUVVIES

A One Act Play

Lynn Brittney

Published by Playstage
United Kingdom

An imprint of Write Publications Ltd

www.playsforadults.com

Designed by Kate Lowe, Greensands Graphics
Printed by Creeds Ltd, Bridport, Dorset

Note to producers about staging "The Luvvies"

This is a very easy play to stage as it is no more than a long table with eight chairs around it, so that all the actors face the audience. Movement is created by the actors coming and going; eating and drinking and changing places. The rest of the drama groups referred to in the script are supposed to be in the direction of the audience, so the actors on stage look out and react to events supposedly happening in that direction.

The pace, particularly during the periods when questions are being asked, should be rapid, with quick-fire responses, but not so fast that the audiences are not able to appreciate the confusion between answering the questions and the management of the swearing list.

The producer should decide in which direction the Quizmaster, or Voice on the Microphone is located so that when there is action by that character, or remarks addressed to that character, the actors on stage always look and speak to the same direction.

Offstage noise from other "drama groups" can be done live or as recorded material. The problem with it being done live is that the sounds will obviously be coming from backstage and not from the direction in which the actors are looking. Therefore, cues for sound effects are provided in the back of this book.

WINE AND WISDOM 2 : THE LUVVIES

CAST *(In order of appearance)*

JUNE	"Leading actress" of the group, age 50+
EILEEN	Very organised and pedantic lady, age 50+
ROGER	Flamboyant male "luvvie", age 50+
MIKE	Slightly irritable with a chip on his shoulder, age 40+
DEBBIE	Neurotic and has allergies, age 40+
TINA	A bit of an air-head, age 35+
PATSY	Harassed housewife, age 40+
SHIRLEY	Nice helpful woman, volunteers for things, age 50+

THE VOICE OF THE QUIZ MASTER

6 female and 3 male parts (including the offstage voice)

The action takes place at the third annual Horbridge Amateur Dramatic Societies Guild Quiz Night.

WINE AND WISDOM 2
THE LUVVIES

There are two tables put together with eight chairs around the tables, so that all the quiz team is facing the audience. JUNE is sitting with EILEEN and they are putting plastic bowls on the table in front of them and filling them up with "nibbles". EILEEN has a bottle of sparkling mineral water and a glass, JUNE has a bottle of red wine and a glass next to her.

JUNE ...so I did, I told her there and then, that I was not going to put up with it. She would just have to find someone else for the part. I told her "I am not kissing that man – not ever. He reeks of drink and cigars and it's just revolting."

EILEEN So what did she say?

JUNE Well, she was very nice about it and she said, of course, that she didn't have anybody else to play the part – my part – but she would see if Roger was available to play the male lead.

EILEEN So what's she going to say to Derek?

JUNE Oh, it's alright. She hasn't offered him the part yet. She wanted to check with me first.

EILEEN I don't even know why she would consider him anyway. He gets so drunk that he never remembers his lines...

JUNE ... and he disrupts rehearsals...Oh do you remember what it was like when we were doing "The Lion in Winter"?

EILEEN Yes.

JUNE	He was so nasty all the time, because his doctor had made him give up drinking. I never want to go through that again. Where is everybody? We said we were going to be here at seven thirty and it's ten to eight now.
EILEEN	Well you know that everyone is always late for everything. We haven't started a rehearsal on time for years. Oh here's Roger!
	(ROGER enters carrying a plastic bag.)
ROGER	Hello my darlings! *(Gives them both a loud kiss)* Sorry I'm late.
JUNE	No Sarah?
ROGER	Alas no. Up all night with sweats and hot flushes again. Feeling like a limp rag. Just didn't feel up to it.
JUNE	Poor Sarah. She is going through it isn't she?
ROGER	She is. Still, you have me, and my encyclopaedic knowledge of the cinema and the female menopause.
EILEEN	Why are they doing the whole quiz about films? I mean, here we are, a collection of twelve drama groups and we should be doing a quiz night about the theatre, shouldn't we?
ROGER	*(Sitting down and getting his wine and stuff out of his bag)* Well my darling, I think that is because the younger members of the Horbridge Amateur Dramatic Society Guild don't go to the theatre.
JUNE	Don't be silly!
ROGER	I kid you not. They go to the "movies" but they don't go to the theatre. They wouldn't know your Noel Coward from your Harold Pinter, my old love. So we can't do a whole

evening's quiz about something they know nothing about, can we?

EILEEN   It's ridiculous. How can you be in a drama group and not go to the theatre?

ROGER   Because they're in a drama group to show off and to find themselves a boyfriend or girlfriend.

JUNE   That's why we never keep any youngsters in our group. We're all too old. They come along for a play reading, take one look at all us geriatrics and never come back again.

EILEEN   That's not true. We've kept Debbie, Tina and Mike.

JUNE   Do you realise that our "juvenile leads" are all over forty!?! I mean they may seem young to you but they're all over forty.

EILEEN   God that makes me feel so old.

ROGER   Join the club dear. Is anyone else coming?

JUNE   Patsy...

ROGER   Oh that's good – she knows everything, bless her...

JUNE   Debbie, Tina and Mike.

ROGER   Ah, the juveniles.

JUNE   That's it. As we have no Sarah, we will have to make do with a team of seven.

ROGER   I thought I saw Shirley when I came in?

EILEEN   Oh yes, but she's just helping with the food and the raffle. She's not on a team.

ROGER   Right, well we should be fine. Ah, I can see the Dalbridge Strollers team arriving.

JUNE	Oh my God! What is Hazel wearing?
EILEEN	I doubt if that skirt could get much shorter.
ROGER	I think it looks very nice. She's got good legs.
JUNE	Roger, she's fifty seven years old and she dresses like an eighteen year old tart!
EILEEN	Did you see her in their last pantomime?
ROGER	Ah yes. I did.
JUNE	Well then, you know how ridiculous she looked.
ROGER	Well I don't know about ridiculous. I was about worried about whether her tits were going to stay in her costume or not. I can't remember much about the story.
JUNE	She's a slut. *(She suddenly changes her face, puts on an expansive smile and stands up)* Cooee! Hazel! Hello darling! Love your outfit! Hello Bob sweetie! What's your next show? *(Pause)* Oh brilliant! I'll look forward to it! *(She sits down again)* Jesus! "Gypsy", for God's sake! No prizes for guessing who's going to be playing Gipsy Rose Lee the stripper.
ROGER	I must book tickets immediately.
	(DEBBIE, TINA and MIKE come in, carrying their plastic bags.)
MIKE	Sorry we're late. We had to go back to Debbie's.
DEBBIE	I forgot my inhaler. I can't risk being out without my inhaler.
TINA	Jesus, it's packed in here, isn't it?
JUNE	Yep. Every single drama group in the Guild has managed to scrape together a team, so it's a bit of a squash. Anyone seen Patsy?

MIKE	Yes. She's just parking her car. She'll be here in a moment.
TINA	Mind you, the car park's absolutely jammed full. I don't know where she's going to find a space.
	(DEBBIE, MIKE and TINA sit down and start to unpack their bags.)
DEBBIE	Actually, can I sit over there next to Roger? Only Tina's got Passion on and it's going to give me a migraine, I know it is.
TINA	Sorry, I forgot.
ROGER	What? Tina's got passion? What?
JUNE	Calm down dear. Tina's wearing the perfume "Passion". Debbie is saying that it gives her a migraine.
ROGER	Oh.
JUNE	I'll swap with you, Debbie. You sit here in-between Eileen and Roger. You'll be fine. Eileen's only perfume is carbolic soap and Roger hasn't washed for weeks. Mike, you sit next to Eileen, and Tina and I will keep our exotic perfumes up this end here. OK? *(They all change seats)*
DEBBIE	Sorry to be a nuisance but you know what I'm like.
ROGER	Yes we do dear. Are any other ailments coming to the fore tonight?
EILEEN	Roger!
DEBBIE	Not at the moment.
	(PATSY arrives, looking harassed, and without a plastic bag)
PATSY	Sorry I'm late. David came home late 'cos the trains were up the creek. Sally's got earache and we had a power cut before I came out.

TINA	Really! Was it the whole area?
PATSY	I think so.
TINA	Damn! I'd set the DVD before I came out. That'll be ruined now.
DEBBIE	Did you find a parking space, Patsy?
PATSY	Just. I'm almost in the field. I'm right on the edge of the car park, in the mud. I hope I can get out again.
JUNE	Sit down love and get yourself a drink.
PATSY	(Clasping her forehead) Oh my God! I knew I'd forgotten something! I've left the bag with the wine and crisps on the hall table! Oh sod it!
ROGER	Not to worry my love. There's plenty to go around. And, because my bag was packed yesterday when my menopausal wife was still coming, I have two glasses here and...I have a choice of red or white wine. What would you like?
PATSY	Oh thanks Roger. I'll have a glass of white please. You are a life saver.
ROGER	Come and sit next to me, sweetheart. Then you can help yourself. Everyone move up one. Oh, you're not wearing exotic perfume are you Patsy?
PATSY	What? Er, no. I haven't got any.
ROGER	Fine, then you won't give Debbie a headache. Come and sit. (SHIRLEY appears carrying paper, pencils and a collection tin.)
EVERYONE	Hello Shirl !... How are you?... Hello love! Etc.
SHIRLEY	I'm fine. Sorry I haven't been along to rehearsals recently

but I've been doing some stuff for the church.

MIKE   We've missed you. Especially your home-made biscuits.

SHIRLEY   Aah, that's kind. I might get along next week.

EILEEN   What's the collecting tin for?

SHIRLEY   Ah, well. I asked the President of the Guild if I could raise some money for the church tonight and he said yes. So I'm running a swear box. I find that works quite well at quiz nights.

JUNE   Oh a swear box! It's a shame we haven't got Derek here. After several drinks he usually turns the air blue and you could have made a fortune!

SHIRLEY   Well, I've only got one tin, so I'm going to have to make one of you swear monitor for the evening and collect up all the money.

EVERYONE
EXCEPT
EILEEN   Eileen!

SHIRLEY   Oh yes, that's a good idea. I'll leave it up to you then Eileen shall I?

EILEEN   Righto.

SHIRLEY   I'll be back later to collect up the papers. We're starting in a minute. *(SHIRLEY leaves)*

(A mobile phone rings and everyone, except ROGER dives for their bags/pockets and gets their phones out. It is PATSY's phone.)

PATSY   Is there a problem? Oh good. *(To everyone else)* The power's back on. *(There are murmurs of "good")* You'll have to put your dinner in the microwave. One minute on reheat. OK? Listen, Sally's had some paracetomol syrup so she can't have any more. If her ear is still aching, get her to lay on a warm, not hot, hot water bottle. OK? I'm going to have to put my phone on silent now, 'cos we're about to start. So if you need anything else, can you text me please? Well get Sally to do it. Yes, you can have the wine in the bag on the hall table. OK. Bye. *(She puts the phone on "silent" and puts it on the table in front of her.)* It's always such a big deal when I come out.

JUNE   That's a good idea. I must put my phone on silent. *(Everyone else does the same and puts their phones in front of them. JUNE looks at EILEEN, who is drawing lines on a sheet of paper)* What are you doing?

EILEEN   I'm making a record sheet for Shirley's swear box.

MIKE   A what?

EILEEN   Look, I've made several columns. We'll have one for "bloody stroke bloody hell", the next one can be "bugger"...we'll make number three "sod" and derivatives of sod....

TINA   Such as?

EILEEN   Sod off? Or sodding?

TINA   Right.

MIKE   You should have a column for "bollocks"

EILEEN   Thank you Mike. I shall just write b stroke s.

JUNE   You can't write that. That means bullshit.

EILEEN   Fine then I'll have a column for b several asterisks and s –

and a column for b stroke s. I am not going to have a column for the f word because I hope that no-one in the group uses the f word. We're all far too mature aren't we?

ALL THE WOMEN	Yes.
EILEEN	*(Persisting and looking at MIKE)* Aren't we?
MIKE	Er, yes. Far too mature.
EILEEN	And Roger?
ROGER	What's that my dear?
EILEEN	No-one in this group uses the f word, do they?
ROGER	Not at all.
MIKE	God help us.
EILEEN	And I think we'll have a column for taking the Lord's name in vain, as this is to raise money for the church.
TINA	*(giggling)* Jesus.
EILEEN	Right, so that will be 10p from Mike and 10p from Tina. Cough up.
	(They reluctantly produce the money and hand it over. DEBBIE gets up and hands her mobile phone to ROGER.)
DEBBIE	I've just remembered, It's time for my suppository. My irritable bowel's been playing up again. Can you take my phone Roger? I'm expecting my reflexologist to ring. I need my energy lines balanced. If she rings, tell her I need an appointment, any time tomorrow. OK?
	(DEBBIE leaves and ROGER makes a face and drops the phone on the table as though it is germ-ridden)

JUNE	She's getting worse you know. She's only been here five minutes and we've had three ailments already.
TINA	It's all stress you know.
ROGER	Just as long as she doesn't have anything catching. I mean I am sitting next to her.
EILEEN	I suspect that Debbie doesn't have anything at all. It's all in her mind.
TINA	No, Eileen, you can't say that. I mean the rashes that she gets whenever she comes into contact with polish and aerosols – they're real enough. And the blisters that came out all over her hands when she touches photocopying paper.
JUNE	Yes and then there was the time when she was throwing up all the way through the dress rehearsal because someone accidentally put sweeteners instead of honey in her tea.
EILEEN	I suppose so.
VOICE OVER THE MICROPHONE (OTM)	Right. Ladies and gentlemen, fellow thespians, I would like to welcome you to the third annual Horbridge Amateur Dramatic Societies Guild's Quiz Night, which this year is on the theme of "The Movies"…
EILEEN	Why does everything have to be so Americanised? Why can't he say "the cinema"?
JUNE	Shush.
VOICE OTM	The first round is going to be a quick-fire round. There will be no time to confer with your fellow team mates. I

shall read out a list of twenty famous movies...

EILEEN	*(being pedantic)* Films!
VOICE OTM	They are all two word titles. You have to write down the missing word. Are we ready?
EVERYONE	Yes!
VOICE OTM	Right, here goes.
JUNE	Patsy, you write them down as Roger tells them to you.
ROGER	Oh it's all up to me is it?
TINA	Jesus, yes.
EILEEN	10p.
VOICE OTM	Number one. Billy...
ROGER	Budd.
VOICE OTM	Number two. Broken...
ROGER	Arrow.
VOICE OTM	Number three. Captain...
ROGER	Blood.
VOICE OTM	Number four. Citizen...
ROGER	Kane.
VOICE OTM	Number five. Dirty...
MIKE & ROGER	Harry.
JUNE	Shush. You'll ruin his concentration! *(MIKE glares at her)*
VOICE OTM	Number six. Key...
ROGER	Largo.
VOICE OTM	Number seven. Lost...

ROGER	Horizon.
VOICE OTM	Number eight. Beau...
ROGER	Geste.
VOICE OTM	Number nine. Love...

(ROGER hesitates for a moment)

TINA	Actually.
JUNE	Boat.
PATSY	Story?
ROGER	Yes,yes – story.
TINA	I think it's Actually. *(She is ignored)*
VOICE OTM	Number ten. Paper...
ROGER	Moon.
VOICE OTM	Number eleven. Pal...
ROGER	Joey.
VOICE OTM	Number twelve. True...
MIKE & ROGER	Grit.
JUNE	Shush!
MIKE	Oy, I'm in this bloody team as well.
EILEEN	10p.
MIKE	Make it twenty, so I can say bollocks to you.
EILEEN	Charming.
VOICE OTM	Number thirteen. Sweet...

(Roger hesitates)

TINA	Jesus.
EILEEN	10p.
ROGER	Charity.
TINA	I know it's for charity.
VOICE OTM	Number fourteen. Magnum…
MIKE & ROGER	Force.
MIKE	Don't say shush or I'll belt you one.
JUNE	Charming.
VOICE OTM	Number fifteen. Midnight…
ROGER	Lace.
PATSY	Never heard of it.
ROGER	Doris Day at her most luscious.
VOICE OTM	Number sixteen. Summer…
EVERYONE	Holiday!
JUNE	Sorry.
EILEEN	Sorry.
ROGER	It's OK.
VOICE OTM	Number seventeen. Easy…
ROGER	Rider.
VOICE OTM	Number eighteen. Bus…
ROGER	Stop.
VOICE OTM	Number nineteen. Elmer…
ROGER	Gantry.

VOICE OTM	And number twenty. Star…
ROGER	Wars?
MIKE	Trek.
TINA	Is born?
PATSY	That's not two words. It's got to be Star Wars or Star Trek.
JUNE	Could be either.
PATSY	Can we have a decision please? Shirley is approaching.
EILEEN	Those in favour of Wars.
	(ROGER, EILEEN and JUNE put their hands up.)
EILEEN	Three. Trek?
	(PATSY, TINA and MIKE put their hands up. DEBBIE comes back)
EILEEN	Three again. Debbie – Star Wars or Star Trek? Quick-choose one.
DEBBIE	What? Oh, er, Star Wars.
	(MIKE tuts and looks annoyed. DEBBIE sits down.)
DEBBIE	Did I miss much?
PATSY	Just a quick-fire round, which Roger demolished fairly quickly.
MIKE	Is it going to be like this all evening? Only if Roger is going to answer all the questions then the rest of us might as well not have come.
JUNE	Oh don't be childish. We just know that Roger is a big film buff, that's all. It was simpler to let him answer all the questions for that quick round.
MIKE	Well just as long as the rest of us get a bloody look-in for

the rest of the evening, that's all.

EILEEN	10p.
MIKE	You are getting on my nerves.
EILEEN	Well then don't swear and I won't irritate you, will I?
TINA	Jesus, Mike. The evening's only just started!
EILEEN	10p
TINA	Oh God!
EILEEN	20p.
MIKE	I don't like being shushed at all the time, that's all.
JUNE	I'm sorry. I won't do it again.
MIKE	Fine.
EILEEN	Tina dear, you owe me 20p for taking the Lord's name in vain, twice.
TINA	Do I? Jesus I didn't realise.
EILEEN	30p.
TINA	What?!
EILEEN	Well, you don't seem to realise how much you say "Jesus". Oh now I'll have to pay 10p.
TINA	Do I? I can't help it.
DEBBIE	*(Starting to cry)* I can't take all these negative emotions. My energy lines are very out of balance, as it is. Now all this conflict is bringing on my asthma. Excuse me, I'll have to go and take a pill. *(She gets up and leaves, sniffling)*
TINA	Now see what you've done.
MIKE	Oh anything sets Debbie off.

JUNE	I'll go and see how she is, I need the loo anyway.
	(JUNE leaves and SHIRLEY arrives)
SHIRLEY	Can I have your answer paper please?
	(PATSY hands it over, SHIRLEY looks at it and gives it back)
SHIRLEY	You haven't put the group's name on the top.
PATSY	Is it just the drama group name? I mean we're not having silly names or anything are we?
SHIRLEY	No just the drama group name.
	(PATSY scribbles the name on the paper and hands it over.)
TINA	How are the other groups doing?
SHIRLEY	Oh not very well, judging by some of the comments I've heard. That first round was a bit of a killer wasn't it?
EILEEN	Not for us. We have Roger.
MIKE	*(testily)* And other people.
SHIRLEY	Oh yes. It looks as though you've probably got them all right. Well done!
ROGER	It was nothing. I had help from others. *(Looks pointedly at MIKE)*
SHIRLEY	How's the collection going?
EILEEN	Well. I have raised £1 so far.
SHIRLEY	Oh lovely! Well I shouldn't say lovely, should I, because it's swearing. But it's good for the church.
EILEEN	Has anyone else raised some money for you?
SHIRLEY	Oh yes. The Theatre Guild Youth Group team has raised five pounds so far.

TINA	But we've only been playing for fifteen minutes!
EILEEN	Yes, well, they're teenagers aren't they? I'm sorry to say that every other word is the f word, from what I can gather.
SHIRLEY	No. It's not from swearing. They just all chipped in and donated five pounds anyway.
TINA	See? You're always ready to judge people harshly, Eileen.
EILEEN	Well, I'm sorry but I can only speak as I find.
PATSY	Don't start having a barney you two. Debbie and Joan are coming back. She'll only break out in a rash if there's another row.
ROGER	How are you Debbie? Feeling any better my love?
DEBBIE	Yes thank you. I took a pill to relax me and I'm feeling much calmer.
TINA	Have some of your wine, love. Eat some of your pumpkin seeds.
ROGER	Oh, you've brought some wine!
DEBBIE	Yes, it's organic Japanese rice wine. It's supposed to be very soothing for the digestion.
ROGER	Pretty powerful stuff I would imagine.
MIKE	I'm just going out for a fag.
ROGER	*(very subtly sarcastic)* Don't be too long Mike. You know we can't do without you.
	(MIKE is about to reply but JUNE glares at him, so he just shrugs his shoulders and slinks off.)
JUNE	I must say, I think Mike is very ratty tonight. More ratty than usual, I would say.

TINA	I think he had a row with his wife before he came out tonight.
JUNE	Oh dear. Is she flexing that thumb of hers again?
TINA	'Fraid so. He doesn't think that he can be in the next production because she kicked up such a stink about him being out at rehearsals for the last one.
JUNE	Mmm. We've been there before, haven't we? I expect he'll have to leave soon. I, for one, can't say that I will be sorry. Mike's a bit too aggressive for my liking. Do you know, the amateur acting world is just like the professional one. Actors should never marry anyone outside the profession. People who are not interested in acting don't understand the level of commitment it requires.
TINA	Oh that's a bit sweeping isn't it? I mean my husband doesn't mind me coming to the drama group twice a week. Neither does Patsy's husband.
JUNE	Yes and that's good. But if you look at all the old-timers. The people who have been in the drama groups for years and years, they are all one half of an acting couple. I mean look at Roger and Sarah., me and George, Eileen and Colin...
EILEEN	Colin hasn't trod the boards for years.
JUNE	No but he did, and that's the important thing. He understands what commitment is required if you truly love acting. There are lots of examples. I mean look at the other groups. There's Hazel and Barry over there...
EILEEN	Except he had an affair with Madge in the Strollers Group and left Hazel for a while...
JUNE	*(ignoring her)* then there's Rita and David, Janice and Peter,

Denise and John…

EILEEN	Yes but didn't Denise used to be married to Peter and John was married to Janice, wasn't he? Weren't they the couples who swapped husbands?
JUNE	Yes, alright! I didn't say that the marriages were perfect! I was just trying to illustrate the point that only another actor understands what is required. You know…whether they're married, dating, committing adultery or what… it's best if it's with another actor.
EILEEN	I'll take your word for that.
VOICE OTM	Right ladies and gentlemen! Time presses on and we need to start round two, otherwise we won't get home tonight!

(MIKE comes rushing in and sits down)

MIKE	I heard the microphone outside.
VOICE OTM	This round is all about musicals.

(There is general approval from everyone except MIKE.)

MIKE	I know sod all about musicals, so I might as well go out for another fag.
EILEEN	You'll give me your 10p before you go, won't you?

(MIKE throws 10p down on the table and stomps off in a huff)

TINA	I hope he doesn't get the hump too much and decide to go home. Debbie and I won't have a lift if he does.
ROGER	Never fear ladies. I will take you home if that happens.
DEBBIE	Thank you Roger. I might ask you to do that anyway. Mike's car smells of burnt-out cigarettes and it makes me feel nauseous. Mm.. this rice wine is nice…

ROGER	I should go easy on it if I were you.
VOICE OTM	Is everyone ready?
JUNE	Patsy, you carry on writing everything down. Your handwriting is so clear.
PATSY	OK.
VOICE OTM	This is a ten question round. Number one. Which musical is set in a Scottish village which only appears every hundred years?
PATSY	I know this one. Its…
	(Offstage we hear another group laughing and all singing "How are things in Glocamorra?")
PATSY	Brigadoon.
JUNE	Which, of course, everyone knows now thanks to Hazel and her group being completely drunk by round two. How typical.
VOICE OTM	Yes thank you Hazel. Question two. Which musical took the music from Borodin's score for Prince Igor?
EILEEN	Ooh..ooh..ooh. I heard that on the radio the other day. It's Kismet.
VOICE OTM	Question three. Which musical is set in Nazi Germany in the 1930's?
	(The drunken HAZEL offstage starts singing "Life is a cabaret, old friend, life is a cabaret.")
JUNE	She is never going to let anyone forget that she played Sally Bowles in Cabaret, is she?
ROGER	It was pretty memorable.
JUNE	Only because, as usual, Hazel did the whole show with

	barely any clothes on.
ROGER	Like I said, it was pretty memorable.
TINA	Oh look, the President's having a word with Hazel and her team. I think he's telling them off.
DEBBIE	I should think so too. They're going to ruin this evening for everyone if they don't stop being silly.
TINA	Oh Jesus, look! She's snogging the President!
JUNE	Disgusting.
EILEEN	10p Tina.
VOICE OTM	Right. The group that were giving you all the musical clues have apologised and said that they won't do it again. But if they do, I may have to have another apology Hazel...
	(There is raucous laughter from offstage.)
JUNE	*(sighing)* Get on with it man!
VOICE OTM	So here we go with question 4. What was the name of the only musical in which Clint Eastwood appeared?
ROGER	Clint Eastwood?!
PATSY	Yes,yes. He was in that one with Lee Marvin....
ROGER	Lee Marvin?! Good God I must have missed that one.
EILEEN	10p Roger.
PATSY	Paint Your Wagon! That's it!
DEBBIE	Well done Patsy.
VOICE OTM	Question Five. Name the musical that only starred children – no adults at all.
	(Everyone looks blank.)
TINA	Oliver?

PATSY	No. That had grown ups in it.
EILEEN	So did the Sound of Music.
JUNE	No idea. Roger?
ROGER	Don't ask me. Musicals are not my forte.
PATSY	We'll leave it and go back to it.
VOICE OTM	Question six. What was the name of the musical film in which "White Christmas" was first sung? First sung. There were two films. I want the first one.
DEBBIE	Oh shit, I think we're going to do badly in this round.
JUNE	Debbie said a bad word Eileen.
EILEEN	I know, but she's thrown me, because I don't have a column for s..h..one..t.
ROGER	Oh well you can't make her pay then.
EILEEN	I'm making a column now. I'll let it go this once but if anyone else uses that word, I'll have them.
JUNE	She's so nit-picking.
VOICE OTM	Question seven. Which musical contains the song "If ever I would leave you."?
JUNE	Oh that's My Fair Lady.
PATSY	No it's not.
JUNE	It is. It's the one sung by the bloke who loves the girl but he doesn't get her in the end.
PATSY	No it's not. He sings "On the street where you live."
JUNE	Then what is it?
PATSY	I dunno. But it's not My Fair Lady. Go back to it.
DEBBIE	*(whispering loudly)* I'm going to text my mum. She'll

	know. *(She starts texting frantically)*
EILEEN	You can't do that, it's cheating!
DEBBIE	No, it's not. She's the eighth member of our team..isn't she Roger?
ROGER	Wizard idea old girl! That rice wine must be perking up your brain cells!
VOICE OTM	Question eight. Which musical is about a Shakespearian play?
VOICE OFFSTAGE	There's two! Which one?
VOICE OTM	Sorry – there's two? Could you come up here and tell me privately? Wait a minute everyone, while we sort this out.
ROGER	Right. While they have a conflab, we can get the answer to the last question from Debbie's mum.
PATSY	Right. The last one. The not My Fair Lady one.
JUNE	I still think it is.
PATSY	No it's not. I can see the bloke singing it. Not your usual musical actor. The one who was in Harry Potter. You know – the one who died.
TINA	Kenneth Branagh?
DEBBIE	He's not dead is he?!
TINA	Oh no, sorry. I was still thinking about the Shakespeare one.
DEBBIE	Eh?
TINA	The one they're arguing about. The Shakespearian one. Never mind.
ROGER	Debbie...your phone is moving across the table!
DEBBIE	Well done mum! She says it's "Camelot."

EVERYONE	Yes!
PATSY	Right. That's that one sorted, now the one about the children's musical.
ROGER	Absolutely no idea. Patsy, you're the only one here with school age children – don't you know?
PATSY	No. My kids don't watch musicals. Nobody kills anybody in musicals.
DEBBIE	I doubt that my mum would know that one. I could try though…
	(MIKE returns)
MIKE	Is it over?
JUNE	No. They've got a small problem, so we're just waiting. Here, you've got kids. What musical film only stars kids and has no adults in it.
MIKE	*(pauses and thinks)* Bugsy Malone?
EVERYONE	That's it….well done…of course it is…etc.
VOICE OTM	Right. We've sorted out the problem and I am going to rephrase the question.
	Question eight. West Side Story was a musical based on a Shakespearian play. Which other musical film is based on a play by Shakespeare and includes scenes from the play?
ROGER	Damn – why couldn't they have given us the other one. I know West Side Story but I haven't a clue about the other one.
EILEEN	I'm going to have to make another column now, as Roger has just come up with another curse.
ROGER	What did I say?

EILEEN	D..A..M..N.
ROGER	That's not swearing!
EILEEN	It's a curse. It's been a curse since medieval times.
ROGER	Great. Are you going to fine me if I say "Zounds!" or "By the Lord Harry!"?
EILEEN	Don't be silly.
MIKE	I don't think Roger is the one being silly.
VOICE OTM	Question nine….
PATSY	Oh God, we haven't written anything down for question eight!
EILEEN	10p.
MIKE	*(to EILEEN)* You're about this far away from death, do you know that?
VOICE OTM	Which musical features a pair of ruby slippers?
MIKE	Wizard of Oz.
TINA	God, that was quick Mike! Well done.
EILEEN	I have an announcement to make.
	(Groans from everyone else)
	I'm only trying to do the job that Shirley asked me to do. But it obviously is making me very unpopular. So I'm not going to say anything more. When you swear, I'm just going to write your initial in one of the columns and total it up at the end. Right?
EVERYONE	*(sulkily)* Right…Yeah…whatever…etc.
EILEEN	I think some of you are being very unfair but that's all I'm going to say on the matter.

VOICE OTM	And the final question. Number ten. Which musical features the song "Who wants to be a millionaire?"
EILEEN	*(huffily)* I know the answer, if anyone is interested.
PATSY	Come on Eileen. Don't get the hump. What is it?
EILEEN	High Society.
ROGER	Yes. Remake of the Philadelphia Story. Well done old girl.
PATSY	It's just the Shakespeare one that we haven't done. Any ideas.
EVERYONE	No...no idea...not a clue...not me..etc.
PATSY	Right. Well we'll just have to forget that one.
DEBBIE	I'll text my mum again. *(She starts texting again)* Would anyone like a pumpkin seed?
ROGER	No thanks, I prefer peanuts.
MIKE	I'll try one. What do pumpkin seeds do for you then?
DEBBIE	Good for your hair....good for your skin...keep your bowels regular...lots of things.
JUNE	Should you eat so much roughage, if you've got irritable bowel syndrome?
DEBBIE	Oh yes. It's vital.
JUNE	*(not convinced)* Right.
DEBBIE	I'm having colonic irrigation next week.
TINA	What's that then?
DEBBIE	Well, they put a tube up your back passage and flush out all the debris.
EVERYONE	Oh my God!...how revolting....disgusting....do you mind!...etc.

ROGER	That's put me right off my peanuts.
DEBBIE	Oh it's very good. Do you know that the body can hang on to stuff for months. It's just there inside you, rotting away, doing terrible things to your system.
EILEEN	I need to go to the toilet.
MIKE	We'll try not to use profane language while you're away.
EILEEN	June, as you are the person who has sworn the least, would you please take over the list in my absence?
JUNE	OK.
	(EILEEN leaves)
JUNE	You shouldn't be so mean to her, you know. She just does her best all the time. She can't help being a perfectionist.
MIKE	She's a pain in the ass.
TINA	Jesus, she can be irritating!
JUNE	I'm marking you down for that, Tina.
TINA	Oh God! I can't help it! I told her!
JUNE	Marking you down again.
MIKE	Bollocks, bollocks, bollocks, bollocks, bollocks, bollocks, bollocks.
JUNE	*(scribbling frantically)* You little git. Was that six or seven times?
MIKE	Bollocks. I meant to make it eight. And while you're there, make a new column.
JUNE	For what?
TINA	You said G..I..T. Eileen didn't make a column for that one.

JUNE	*(laughing)* So she didn't!
PATSY	Here, while you're at it, make some more new columns. She'll be horrified when she comes back.
JUNE	What am I going to put in them?
ROGER	You could make one for Gordon Bennett.
PATSY	Do one for Gawblimey.
MIKE	How about "cow son"?
JUNE	What?
MIKE	Yeah, you know, like that Chas and Dave song "Gertcha". My grandad used to say it all the time. "Get in you cow son" he used to say, when he couldn't hammer a nail into the wall.
JUNE	I've never heard that one before.
MIKE	Well, you're too middle class aren't you?
DEBBIE	*(giggling)* You should make a column for "asshole."
PATSY	Oy, this is getting a bit too graphic for me, thank you. Can we change the subject? How much have you had to drink by the way?
DEBBIE	Not much. Try some.
PATSY	OK. *(She offers her empty glass. DEBBIE pours in a little rice wine and PATSY tastes it. She coughs and splutters.)* Bloody hell! That's like paint stripper!
JUNE	Oops, quick! Eileen's coming back.
	(EILEEN appears and looks at the swear-list.)
EILEEN	I see you've all enjoyed yourselves while I've been away.
	(There are a few sniggers)

JUNE	Oh come on, Eileen, lighten up. It's just a joke.
EILEEN	It's alright. I'm used to being the butt of jokes.
	(Everyone looks at each other and looks guilty. DEBBIE'S phone vibrates.)
ROGER	Mum is calling again!
DEBBIE	Right. Eh? *(She looks at the phone)* That can't be right! *(She starts giggling)* I must have dialled the wrong number!
TINA	Who is it then?
DEBBIE	Some person who says "Who are you? Is this a wind-up?" I'd better text him to say sorry.
JUNE	Well you can't text your mum again. Shirley's approaching.
	(SHIRLEY enters)
SHIRLEY	Can I have your paper please? You'll be pleased to know that you got a perfect score for the first round.
	(Everyone makes approving noises)
	Oh and it looks like you've done quite well on this round as well. Keep up the good work. *(SHIRLEY leaves)*
VOICE OTM	Right, now round three is about science fiction films.
	(There are groans from everywhere. ROGER looks disgusted but MIKE looks happy.)
MIKE	Oh great! This is where I amaze and astound you all.
ROGER	Oh well, I'm glad someone knows about it. I can't stand science fiction films myself. It's about the only genre I hate. Well, except for soppy romantic films.
VOICE OTM	Question one. What is the name of the enemy agent in the film "The Matrix"?

MIKE   Cool.

              (PATSY starts writing)

              No don't write that. I was just saying "Cool." The answer
              is Agent Smith.

PATSY   Oh right.

VOICE OTM   Question two. In the Star Wars Trilogy, what species is the
              character "Chewbacca."

ROGER   This is all like a foreign language to me.

MIKE   He was a Wookey.

PATSY   How do you spell that?

MIKE   W..O..O..K..E..Y.

VOICE OTM   Question three. In Alien, the first film, what was the name
              of the actor who carried the alien inside his stomach?

JUNE   Yuk!

MIKE   Oh yeah, it was great. Splat! When it burst out of his gut it
              was one of the all time greatest movie moments!

EILEEN   Just the thing you want to watch when you're having your tea.

PATSY   So what was his name?

MIKE   Sorry. John Hurt.

TINA   Really? I thought he was a classical actor?

ROGER   No. He was the one who played the pouff.

JUNE   What pouff?

ROGER   You know...Crisp.

JUNE   Oh Quentin Crisp! Yes, I remember.

VOICE OTM   Question four. In Logan's Run. What colour did the hand crystal turn, when a person reached the age of thirty?

MIKE Oh shit! I don't know this one.

(EILEEN marks the sheet. MIKE gets ratty)

Please don't do that.

EILEEN Pardon?

MIKE I can see you marking that bloody sheet. Please don't do it.

(She slowly and deliberately marks the sheet again, in the "bloody" column and then stares at him defiantly.)

MIKE You are going to be so sorry that you did that.

EILEEN Please don't threaten me.

PATSY Oy, excuse me but I'm waiting for an answer to this question, Mike.

MIKE Well, I can't give you one, alright?

VOICE OTM Question five. In the film Blade Runner, what was the name of the leader of the renegade androids.

PATSY Mike?

MIKE I don't know. I'm not playing any more.

TINA What!

DEBBIE He's giving me bad vibes Roger.

ROGER Look, mate, don't be childish. Just play the game, eh?

MIKE Sod off, mate. I'm not the one being childish here.

(He grabs EILEEN'S pencil and snaps it in half)

I can't think with you doing that! If you don't stop, I'm going to use the f-word – and the c-word – and any other word I can think of!

VOICE OTM	Question six. What is the name of the film, set on a futuristic mining planet, which was a remake of "High Noon"?
EILEEN	I think I'm going to have to go home.
JUNE	No, Eileen, wait.
	(EILEEN *grabs her bottle of mineral water and her bowl of crisps , puts them in her plastic bag and leaves.*)
JUNE	What did you do that for?
MIKE	She was asking for it.
JUNE	No she wasn't. I know she can be a bit irritating sometimes but you just took it out on her 'cos you couldn't answer the questions.
VOICE OTM	Question seven. In the film…
MIKE	*(shouting)* Can you hang on a minute mate! We've got a bit of a problem here!
TINA	Mike!
VOICE OTM	Sorry? A problem?…
MIKE	*(shouting)* Yeah. Just shut your face for five minutes, will you?
ROGER	Good God!
VOICE OTM	*(sounding confused)* I beg your pardon?
MIKE	You heard me! Just shut it for a minute. We're trying to sort something out here!
ROGER	I think you'd better leave, Mike.
MIKE	Are you going to make me?
JUNE	Don't be ridiculous! I can't believe you would be so

offensive, just because you can't answer a few questions!

VOICE OTM   Could you please take any problems that you have outside…Please consider other people…

MIKE   I'm going to do for him…*(He pushes a chair over as though he is about to start a fight. ROGER leaps up and restrains him. DEBBIE screams.)*

ROGER   Pull yourself together man! This is unacceptable!

MIKE   *(Throwing ROGER off and mimicking his voice)* Oh, this is unacceptable! What a bunch of toffee-nosed snobs! I'm pig-sick of your drama group! You're all a load of talentless has-beens! You can't act to save your lives!

(There is a shocked silence and JUNE stands up with great dignity.)

JUNE   *(speaking quietly, with great authority and getting gradually louder and more imperious)*

How dare you cast aspersions on our acting ability. There are people here tonight who have been acting for over thirty years and given a great many people a great deal of joy. We are true actors. We don't get paid to do it – we often end up spending our own money to put on a production – we work hard all day and then come out in the evenings, often when we are very tired, and rehearse with a level of commitment that you would just not understand. Your idea of acting is to shout a lot and dominate the centre of the stage as though you were the only person on it. You have no concept of team work, you are not generous to other actors, you are disruptive, selfish and rude in rehearsals. Frankly, we do not need someone like you. You are a shallow egotist who refuses to take direction from others more experienced than you and, as a result, you drag the quality of our productions down to your own bombastic, unsubtle level. You are not welcome in our group anymore.

(There is a moment of silence and then the unseen drama groups offstage burst into a round of applause with much foot-stamping and whistling. MIKE looks angry and defeated and leaves. JUNE sways a little and slumps into her chair. The others crowd around to revive her.)

DEBBIE   Have some rice wine!

ROGER   Magnificent old girl! Magnificent!

TINA   Ooh God, June, weren't you frightened?

JUNE   Absolutely terrified! But he made me so angry and when I am angry I get very articulate.

PATSY   We noticed. What a performance!

(EILEEN enters, sheepishly, carrying her plastic bag.)

EILEEN   I was standing at the back of the hall and I heard it all. June, you were wonderful!

JUNE   Thank you dear. Did you see where Mike went?

EILEEN   Yes. He stormed past me, got into his car and left.

VOICE OTM   Well, everyone. Now that we've been treated to a cabaret, as well as a quiz – can we resume?

(Laughter offstage)

VOICE OTM   I think, as time is pressing on, we will forget the last round and move on to the next.

ROGER   Hear, hear!

EILEEN   Shall I continue with Shirley's swear – list?

EVERYONE   No!

JUNE	*(tearing the list up into little pieces)* I say that we all give two pounds into the kitty and forget the bloody swear list. All in favour?
EVERYONE	Aye!
VOICE OTM	This round is all about stage plays that have been made into movies...
EILEEN	*(loudly)* Films – PLEASE!
VOICE OTM	Sorry?
EILEEN	I beg your pardon Mr President, but we are not American. Could you please say "films" and not "movies"?
	(Groans from offstage)
TINA	We're going to get a reputation for being difficult...
JUNE	Eileen, stop being so nit-picking! You're obsessive! We take one thing away from you and you find something else to be pedantic about.
EILEEN	Sorry.
VOICE OTM	OK. I have conferred with fellow committee members and we have agreed to change the word "movies" into "films" – provided that there are no more interruptions from that group over there...
EVERYONE	Promise!...Sorry...Absolutely...etc.
VOICE OTM	Right. Eyes down. Pencils poised. Question Number One. A famous Agatha Christie stage play was made into a film which starred Marlene Dietrich and Tyrone Power. What was the film called?

BLACKOUT   * END OF PLAY *

FURNITURE LIST

Throughout: one long table, or two tables pushed togethers, and eight chairs arranged around the ends and upstage side of the table/s.

PROPERTY LIST

Page 1:   JUNE: is already on stage with a bottle of red wine; a glass; a plastic bowl; a large bag of crisps, a carrier bag and a handbag which contains coins – 10p, 20p and £2, mobile phone.

EILEEN: is already on stage with a bottle of sparkling mineral water; a glass; plastic bowl and a large bag of peanuts; handbag; carrier bag; 10p, 20p and £1 coins.

Page 2:   ROGER: enters with a carrier bag containing two bottles of wine; two glasses; savoury "nibbles", coins – 10p, 20p, £1.

Page 4:   DEBBIE : enters with a carrier bag containing a bottle of rice wine; bag of pumpkin seeds; plastic bowl; glass; handbag containing mobile phone; inhaler; bottle of pills; packet of suppositories and 10p, 20p and £1 coins.

TINA : enters with a carrier bag; bottle of wine, glass, bag of crisps; handbag containing mobile phone and 10p, 20p and £1 coins.

MIKE: enters with carrier bag containing four cans of lager; packet of cigarettes; lighter; bag of peanuts *(no bowl).* In his jacket pocket he has a mobile phone and lots of 10p and 20p coins.

Page 5:   PATSY: enters with a handbag containing a mobile phone and 10p, 20p and £1 coins. *(No carrier bag of wine and snacks.)*

Page 6:   SHIRLEY: enters with a wad of paper; eight pencils and a collecting tin or box.

LIGHTING PLOT

Music should be faded before the lights are brought up, as the actors start the play in mid-conversation.

Basically, bring up lights gradually to normal range on Page 1 of the script and quick blackout at the end, bringing in the music at full volume on the last line of Page 35.

EFFECTS PLOT

The VOICE OVER THE MICROPHONE should really be done live by an actor backstage on a microphone. It is possible that you could do the crowd sound effects live, if you had a microphone set up in a separate room so that both the VOICE OTM and a group of other actors could use it. It would have to be carefully managed though. However, in case you decide to record the effects, the cues are given below.

Page 7:	CUE: SHIRLEY…We're starting in a minute… *(SHIRLEY leaves)* *A mobile phone rings.*
Page 20:	CUE: PATSY…I know this one. Its… *Sounds of people laughing and singing "How Are Things in Glocomorra?"*
Page 20:	CUE: VOICE OTM…which musical is set in Nazi Germany in the 1930's?… *Woman's voice singing "Life is a cabaret old friend, life is a cabaret"* *Laughter from crowd.*
Page 21:	CUE: VOICE OTM…I may have to have another apology from Hazel… *Raucous laughter from crowd.*
Page 29:	CUE: VOICE OTM…round three is about science fiction films… *Groans from crowd.*
Page 34:	CUE: JUNE…You are not welcome in our group any more… *Round of applause, with whistling and cheering.*
Page 35:	CUE: EILEEN…please say "films" and not "movies"… *Groans from the crowd.*